Eggs Around the Globe

75 Recipes from Around the World

Table of contents

34. Indian Egg Biryani
35. Moroccan B'stilla (savoury pie with eggs)
36. Chinese Tea Eggs (Marbled Eggs)
37. Turkish Cilbir (Poached Eggs in Yogurt)
38. Nigerian Egg Stew
39. Cuban Huevos Habaneros
40. Thai Khai Yad Sai (Stuffed Eggs)
41. Australian Avocado Toast with Poached Egg
42. Japanese Onsen Tamago (Soft-Boiled Eggs)
43. Korean Bibimbap with Fried Egg
44. Egyptian Koshari with Fried Egg
45. Brazilian Pão de Queijo with Egg
46. Mexican Migas
47. Italian Eggplant Parmesan
48. Greek Avgolemono Soup
49. Turkish Manti with Yogurt and Egg
50. Spanish Migas with Chorizo and Egg
51. Thai Khai Jiao Khanom Pang (Egg Toast)
52. Moroccan Mealmen with Egg
53. Nigerian Egg Roll
54. Indonesian Nasi Goreng with Egg
55. Brazilian Coxinha de Galinha (Chicken Croquette with Egg)
56. Lebanese Fatteh with Egg
57. Italian Eggplant Involtini
58. Korean Japchae with Egg
59. Mexican Tacos de Papa con Huevo (Potato and Egg Tacos)
60. Chinese Century Egg Congee
61. Thai Kai Look Kuey (Son-in-Law Eggs)
62. Vietnamese Bánh Mì with Fried Egg
63. Indian Egg Korma
64. Turkish Börek with Egg
65. French Croque Madame
66. Nigerian Moi Moi (Steamed Bean Pudding with Egg)
67. Egyptian Hawawshi with Egg
68. Lebanese Knafeh with Egg

69. Spanish Patatas a la Riojana with Egg
70. Thai Khai Khem (Salted Eggs)
71. Brazilian Brigadeiro with Egg
72. Mexican Tlacoyo with Egg
73. Italian Eggplant Caponata
74. Nigerian Akara (Bean Fritters with Egg)
75. Lebanese Manakish with Egg
76. Korean Kimchi Fried Rice with Egg
77. Thai Pad See Ew with Egg
78. Brazilian Pamonha with Egg
79. Italian Tiramisu
80. Indian Egg Curry

1. Spanish Tortilla de Patatas:

- Preparation Time: 15 minutes
- Cooking Time: 30 minutes
- Serves: 4

Ingredients:
- 4 large potatoes, peeled and thinly sliced
- 1 onion, thinly sliced
- 6 eggs
- Salt and pepper to taste
- Olive oil

Instructions:
1. Heat a generous amount of olive oil in a non-stick skillet over medium heat.
2. Add the sliced potatoes and onions to the skillet. Cook, stirring occasionally, until the potatoes are tender and lightly golden, about 10-15 minutes. Season with salt and pepper.
3. In a separate bowl, beat the eggs and season with salt and pepper.
4. Once the potatoes are cooked, transfer them to the bowl with the beaten eggs and mix well.
5. Heat a little more olive oil in the skillet over medium heat. Pour the potato and egg mixture into the skillet and spread it out evenly.
6. Cook the tortilla for about 5-7 minutes on each side, until golden brown and set in the centre.
7. Slide the tortilla onto a plate and allow it to cool slightly before slicing into wedges. Serve warm or at room temperature.

Serving Suggestion: Serve with a side of crusty bread and a simple green salad for a complete meal.

2. French Omelette:

- Preparation Time: 5 minutes
- Cooking Time: 5 minutes
- Serves: 1

Ingredients:
- 3 large eggs
- Salt and pepper to taste
- Butter or olive oil

Instructions:
1. Crack the eggs into a bowl and beat them lightly with a fork. Season with salt and pepper.
2. Heat a small non-stick skillet over medium heat and add a knob of butter or a drizzle of olive oil.
3. Once the butter has melted or the oil is hot, pour the beaten eggs into the skillet.
4. Using a spatula, gently push the cooked edges of the omelette towards the centre, tilting the skillet to allow the uncooked eggs to flow to the edges.
5. Continue cooking until the eggs are set but still slightly runny on top, about 2-3 minutes.
6. Fold the omelette in half using the spatula and slide it onto a plate. Serve immediately.

Serving Suggestion: Garnish with fresh herbs such as chives or parsley, and serve with a side of toast or sautéed vegetables.

3. Italian Frittata:

- Preparation Time: 10 minutes
- Cooking Time: 15 minutes
- Serves: 4

Ingredients:
- 6 large eggs
- 1/2 cup grated Parmesan cheese
- Salt and pepper to taste
- 1 tablespoon olive oil
- Fillings of your choice (e.g., cooked vegetables, meats, cheeses)

Instructions:
1. Preheat the broiler in your oven.
2. In a large bowl, beat the eggs and stir in the grated Parmesan cheese. Season with salt and pepper.
3. Heat the olive oil in an oven-safe skillet over medium heat. Add your chosen fillings and cook until heated through.
4. Pour the beaten eggs over the fillings in the skillet, making sure they are evenly distributed.
5. Cook the frittata on the stovetop for 5-7 minutes, until the edges begin to set.
6. Transfer the skillet to the preheated broiler and cook for an additional 5-7 minutes, until the top is golden brown and the eggs are set in the centre.
7. Remove the frittata from the oven and let it cool slightly before slicing into wedges. Serve warm or at room temperature.

Serving Suggestion: Serve with a side of mixed greens dressed with balsamic vinaigrette for a light and flavorful meal.

4. American Eggs Benedict:
- Preparation Time: 15 minutes
- Cooking Time: 15 minutes
- Serves: 2

Ingredients:
- 4 large eggs
- 2 English muffins, split and toasted
- 4 slices Canadian bacon or ham
- Hollandaise sauce (homemade or store-bought)
- Salt and pepper to taste
- Chopped fresh parsley for garnish (optional)

Instructions:
1. Fill a large skillet with water and bring it to a gentle simmer over medium heat. Add a splash of white vinegar to the water.
2. Crack each egg into a small bowl or ramekin. Carefully slide the eggs, one at a time, into the simmering water. Poach the eggs for 3-4 minutes, until the whites are set but the yolks are still runny.
3. While the eggs are poaching, heat a separate skillet over medium heat and cook the Canadian bacon or ham slices until heated through.
4. To assemble, place a toasted English muffin half on each plate. Top each muffin half with a slice of Canadian bacon or ham, followed by a poached egg.

5. Drizzle Hollandaise sauce over each egg, and season with salt and pepper to taste. Garnish with chopped fresh parsley if desired.

6. Serve immediately, with additional Hollandaise sauce on the side if desired.

Serving Suggestion: Serve with a side of roasted asparagus or steamed broccoli for a classic brunch dish.

5. Turkish Menemen:

- Preparation Time: 10 minutes
- Cooking Time: 15 minutes
- Serves: 2

Ingredients:
- 4 large eggs
- 2 tomatoes, diced
- 1 onion, thinly sliced
- 1 green bell pepper, diced
- 2 cloves garlic, minced
- 2 tablespoons olive oil
- 1 teaspoon paprika
- Salt and pepper to taste
- Fresh parsley, chopped, for garnish

Instructions:

1. Heat the olive oil in a large skillet over medium heat. Add the sliced onion and diced green bell pepper, and sauté until softened, about 5 minutes.

2. Add the minced garlic to the skillet and cook for an additional 1-2 minutes, until fragrant.

3. Stir in the diced tomatoes and paprika, and season with salt and pepper to taste. Cook for another 5 minutes, until the tomatoes have softened and released their juices.

4. Using a spoon, make small wells in the tomato mixture and crack an egg into each well. Season the eggs with salt and pepper.

5. Cover the skillet and cook for 5-7 minutes, until the egg whites are set but the yolks are still runny.

6. Remove the skillet from the heat and sprinkle with chopped fresh parsley. Serve immediately.

Serving Suggestion: Serve with crusty bread or warm flatbread for scooping up the flavorful tomato and egg mixture.

6. Chinese Egg Fried Rice:

- Preparation Time: 10 minutes
- Cooking Time: 10 minutes
- Serves: 4

Ingredients:
- 4 cups cooked rice (preferably day-old)
- 3 eggs, beaten
- 2 tablespoons vegetable oil
- 1 cup mixed vegetables (such as peas, carrots, and corn)
- 2 cloves garlic, minced
- 2 tablespoons soy sauce
- Salt and pepper to taste
- Green onions, thinly sliced, for garnish

Instructions:
1. Heat the vegetable oil in a large skillet or wok over medium-high heat.

2. Add the minced garlic and cook for about 30 seconds, until fragrant.

3. Add the beaten eggs to the skillet and scramble them until they are cooked through.

4. Add the cooked rice and mixed vegetables to the skillet, stirring to combine.

5. Pour the soy sauce over the rice mixture and continue to cook, stirring frequently, until everything is heated through.
6. Season with salt and pepper to taste.
7. Garnish with sliced green onions before serving.

Serving Suggestion: Serve hot as a main dish or as a side dish with your favourite Chinese entrees.

7. Japanese Tamagoyaki:

- Preparation Time: 5 minutes
- Cooking Time: 10 minutes
- Serves: 2-4

Ingredients:
- 4 large eggs
- 2 tablespoons dashi (Japanese soup stock)
- 1 tablespoon soy sauce
- 1 teaspoon sugar
- Salt to taste
- Vegetable oil for cooking

Instructions:
1. In a bowl, beat the eggs and whisk in the dashi, soy sauce, sugar, and salt until well combined.
2. Heat a tamagoyaki pan or a small non-stick skillet over medium heat and brush it with a thin layer of vegetable oil.
3. Pour a thin layer of the egg mixture into the pan, tilting to spread it evenly.
4. Once the bottom is set but the top is still slightly runny, roll the egg from one end of the pan to the other using chopsticks or a spatula.

5. Push the rolled egg to one side of the pan and brush the empty side with more oil. Pour another thin layer of the egg mixture into the pan, lifting the rolled egg slightly to let the new layer flow underneath.

6. Roll the egg again when the bottom is set but the top is still slightly runny.

7. Repeat this process until all the egg mixture is used up and you have a neat, cylindrical shape.

8. Transfer the rolled egg to a cutting board and let it cool slightly before slicing into rounds.

Serving Suggestion: Serve as a side dish or as part of a traditional Japanese breakfast.

8. Indian Masala Egg Curry:

- Preparation Time: 10 minutes
- Cooking Time: 20 minutes
- Serves: 4

Ingredients:
- 6 hard-boiled eggs, peeled and halved
- 2 tablespoons vegetable oil
- 1 onion, finely chopped
- 2 tomatoes, finely chopped
- 2 teaspoons ginger-garlic paste
- 1 teaspoon ground cumin
- 1 teaspoon ground coriander
- 1/2 teaspoon turmeric powder
- 1/2 teaspoon red chilli powder (adjust to taste)
- 1/2 teaspoon garam masala
- Salt to taste
- Fresh cilantro, chopped, for garnish

Instructions:

1. Heat the vegetable oil in a skillet over medium heat. Add the chopped onion and sauté until translucent.

2. Add the ginger-garlic paste to the skillet and cook for another minute, until fragrant.

3. Add the chopped tomatoes, ground cumin, ground coriander, turmeric powder, red chilli powder, and salt to the skillet. Cook until the tomatoes break down and the mixture thickens.

4. Gently add the halved hard-boiled eggs to the skillet, making sure they are coated in the masala sauce.

5. Cover the skillet and simmer for 5-7 minutes to allow the flavours to meld together.

6. Sprinkle the garam masala over the curry and stir to combine.

7. Garnish with chopped fresh cilantro before serving.

Serving Suggestion: Serve hot with rice or flatbread for a satisfying Indian meal.

9. Mexican Huevos Rancheros:

- Preparation Time: 10 minutes
- Cooking Time: 15 minutes
- Serves: 2

Ingredients:
- 4 large eggs
- 4 corn tortillas
- 1 cup refried beans
- 1 cup salsa
- 1/2 cup shredded cheese (such as cheddar or Monterey Jack)
- 2 tablespoons vegetable oil
- Salt and pepper to taste
- Fresh cilantro, chopped, for garnish

Instructions:
1. Heat the vegetable oil in a skillet over medium heat. Fry the corn tortillas until crisp on both sides, about 1-2 minutes per side. Drain on paper towels.

2. In the same skillet, heat the refried beans until warmed through.

3. Meanwhile, fry the eggs in another skillet to your desired doneness, seasoning with salt and pepper.

4. To assemble, place a fried tortilla on each plate. Spread a layer of refried beans on top of each tortilla.

5. Top each tortilla with a fried egg and spoon salsa over the eggs.

6. Sprinkle shredded cheese over the top and garnish with chopped fresh cilantro.

7. Serve immediately.

Serving Suggestion: Serve with avocado slices, sour cream, and lime wedges for a hearty Mexican breakfast or brunch.

10. Thai Kai Jeow (Thai Omelette):

- Preparation Time: 5 minutes
- Cooking Time: 5 minutes
- Serves: 2-4

Ingredients:
- 4 large eggs
- 2 tablespoons fish sauce
- 1 tablespoon soy sauce
- 1 tablespoon cornstarch
- 2 cloves garlic, minced
- 2 green onions, finely chopped
- Vegetable oil for frying

Instructions:
1. In a bowl, beat the eggs and whisk in the fish sauce, soy sauce, and cornstarch until well combined.

2. Stir in the minced garlic and chopped green onions.

3. Heat a generous amount of vegetable oil in a skillet over medium-high heat.

4. Once the oil is hot, pour the egg mixture into the skillet, spreading it out evenly to form a large omelette.

5. Cook the omelette for 2-3 minutes on one side, until golden brown and crispy.

6. Carefully flip the omelette over and cook for another 1-2 minutes on the other side.

7. Remove the omelette from the skillet and drain on paper towels.

8. Cut the omelette into wedges and serve immediately.

Serving Suggestion: Serve with steamed rice and a dipping sauce made from soy sauce, lime juice, and chilli flakes for a traditional Thai breakfast or as part of a larger meal.

11. Greek Spanakopita:

- Preparation Time: 30 minutes
- Cooking Time: 45 minutes
- Serves: 6-8

Ingredients:
- 1 package (16 ounces) frozen spinach, thawed and drained
- 1 cup crumbled feta cheese
- 1/2 cup grated Parmesan cheese
- 4 green onions, finely chopped
- 2 cloves garlic, minced
- 1/4 cup chopped fresh dill
- Salt and pepper to taste
- 4 large eggs, beaten
- 1/2 cup melted butter
- 12 sheets phyllo dough, thawed
- Olive oil for brushing

Instructions:

1. Preheat the oven to 350°F (175°C). Grease a 9x13-inch baking dish.

2. In a large bowl, combine the drained spinach, feta cheese, Parmesan cheese, green onions, garlic, dill, salt, pepper, and beaten eggs.

3. Lay one sheet of phyllo dough in the prepared baking dish and brush it with melted butter. Repeat with 5 more sheets of phyllo dough, brushing each sheet with melted butter.

4. Spread the spinach and cheese mixture evenly over the phyllo dough.

5. Layer the remaining sheets of phyllo dough over the spinach mixture, brushing each sheet with melted butter.

6. Score the top layer of phyllo dough into squares or triangles with a sharp knife.

7. Bake in the preheated oven for 40-45 minutes, or until the top is golden brown and crispy.

8. Allow the spanakopita to cool for a few minutes before slicing and serving.

Serving Suggestion: Serve warm or at room temperature as a side dish or appetiser with a dollop of Greek yoghurt or tzatziki sauce.

12. Lebanese Shakshuka:

- Preparation Time: 10 minutes
- Cooking Time: 20 minutes
- Serves: 4

Ingredients:
- 2 tablespoons olive oil
- 1 onion, diced
- 2 cloves garlic, minced
- 1 red bell pepper, diced
- 1 yellow bell pepper, diced
- 1 teaspoon ground cumin
- 1 teaspoon smoked paprika
- 1/2 teaspoon cayenne pepper (optional)
- 1 can (14 ounces) diced tomatoes
- 4-6 eggs
- Salt and pepper to taste
- Fresh parsley, chopped, for garnish

Instructions:

1. Heat the olive oil in a large skillet over medium heat. Add the diced onion and cook until softened, about 5 minutes.

2. Add the minced garlic and diced bell peppers to the skillet and cook for another 5 minutes, until the peppers are softened.

3. Stir in the ground cumin, smoked paprika, and cayenne pepper (if using) until fragrant, about 1 minute.

4. Pour in the diced tomatoes with their juices and bring the mixture to a simmer. Cook for 5-10 minutes, until slightly thickened.

5. Using a spoon, create small wells in the tomato mixture and crack an egg into each well.

6. Cover the skillet and cook for 5-7 minutes, until the egg whites are set but the yolks are still runny.

7. Season with salt and pepper to taste and garnish with chopped fresh parsley before serving.

Serving Suggestion: Serve hot with crusty bread for dipping into the flavorful tomato sauce.

13. British Scotch Eggs:

- Preparation Time: 20 minutes
- Cooking Time: 15 minutes
- Serves: 4

Ingredients:
- 4 large eggs
- 1 pound ground pork sausage
- 1/2 cup all-purpose flour
- 1 cup breadcrumbs
- Vegetable oil for frying
- Salt and pepper to taste

Instructions:
1. Place the eggs in a saucepan and cover them with cold water. Bring the water to a boil, then reduce the heat and simmer for 6-7 minutes.

2. Remove the eggs from the saucepan and place them in a bowl of ice water to cool. Once cooled, peel the eggs and set them aside.

3. Divide the ground pork sausage into 4 equal portions. Flatten each portion into a thin patty.

4. Place a peeled egg in the centre of each sausage patty and gently shape the sausage around the egg, making sure it is completely covered.

5. Roll each sausage-covered egg in flour, shaking off any excess.

6. Dip the floured eggs in beaten eggs, then roll them in breadcrumbs until evenly coated.

7. Heat vegetable oil in a deep fryer or large skillet to 350°F (175°C). Carefully add the coated eggs to the hot oil and fry for 5-6 minutes, until golden brown and cooked through.

8. Remove the Scotch eggs from the oil and drain on paper towels. Season with salt and pepper to taste before serving.

Serving Suggestion: Serve hot or at room temperature with your favourite mustard or dipping sauce.

14. Korean Gyeran Jjim (Steamed Egg):

- Preparation Time: 5 minutes
- Cooking Time: 10 minutes
- Serves: 2-4

Ingredients:
- 4 large eggs
- 1 cup water
- 1 tablespoon soy sauce
- 1 teaspoon sesame oil
- Salt to taste
- Chopped scallions for garnish

Instructions:

1. In a bowl, beat the eggs and whisk in the water, soy sauce, sesame oil, and salt until well combined.

2. Strain the egg mixture through a fine mesh sieve into a heatproof bowl or individual serving bowls.

3. Cover the bowl(s) with aluminium foil or a lid.

4. Place the bowl(s) in a steamer basket or pot with simmering water. Steam for 8-10 minutes, until the eggs are set but still slightly jiggly in the centre.

5. Carefully remove the bowl(s) from the steamer and garnish with chopped scallions before serving.

Serving Suggestion: Serve hot as a side dish with steamed rice and other Korean banchan (side dishes).

15. Moroccan Tagine with Eggs:

- Preparation Time: 15 minutes
- Cooking Time: 30 minutes
- Serves: 4

Ingredients:
- 4 large eggs
- 1 onion, finely chopped
- 2 cloves garlic, minced
- 1 red bell pepper, diced
- 1 yellow bell pepper, diced
- 1 can (14 ounces) diced tomatoes
- 1 teaspoon ground cumin
- 1 teaspoon ground paprika

- 1/2 teaspoon ground turmeric
- Salt and pepper to taste
- Fresh cilantro, chopped, for garnish

Instructions:
1. Heat a tablespoon of olive oil in a tagine or large skillet over medium heat. Add the chopped onion and cook until softened, about 5 minutes.
2. Add the minced garlic, diced bell peppers, ground cumin, ground paprika, and ground turmeric to the tagine. Cook for another 5 minutes, until the peppers are softened and the spices are fragrant.
3. Pour in the diced tomatoes with their juices and bring the mixture to a simmer. Cook for 10-15 minutes, until slightly thickened.
4. Using a spoon, create small wells in the tomato mixture and crack an egg into each well.
5. Cover the tagine and cook for 10-12 minutes, until the egg whites are set but the yolks are still runny.
6. Season with salt and pepper to taste and garnish with chopped fresh cilantro before serving.

Serving Suggestion: Serve hot with crusty bread or couscous for a comforting Moroccan meal.

16. Argentine Tortilla Española:
- Preparation Time: 15 minutes
- Cooking Time: 30 minutes
- Serves: 4-6

Ingredients:
- 4 large potatoes, peeled and thinly sliced
- 1 onion, thinly sliced
- 6 large eggs
- Salt and pepper to taste

- Olive oil

Instructions:
1. Heat a generous amount of olive oil in a large skillet over medium heat.
2. Add the sliced potatoes and onions to the skillet. Cook, stirring occasionally, until the potatoes are tender and lightly golden, about 10-15 minutes. Season with salt and pepper.
3. In a separate bowl, beat the eggs and season with salt and pepper.
4. Once the potatoes are cooked, transfer them to the bowl with the beaten eggs and mix well.
5. Heat a little more olive oil in the skillet over medium heat. Pour the potato and egg mixture into the skillet and spread it out evenly.
6. Cook the tortilla for about 5-7 minutes on each side, until golden brown and set in the centre.
7. Slide the tortilla onto a plate and allow it to cool slightly before slicing into wedges. Serve warm or at room temperature.

Serving Suggestion: Serve as a tapa with crusty bread and a glass of red wine.

17. Russian Egg Salad (Salat Olivier):
- Preparation Time: 20 minutes
- Cooking Time: 20 minutes
- Serves: 4-6

Ingredients:
- 4 large potatoes, peeled and diced
- 4 large carrots, peeled and diced
- 4 large eggs

- 1 cup diced cooked ham or bologna
- 1 cup frozen peas, thawed
- 1 cup diced pickles
- 1/2 cup diced onion
- 1/2 cup mayonnaise
- 2 tablespoons Dijon mustard
- Salt and pepper to taste

Instructions:
1. Place the diced potatoes and carrots in a large pot of salted water. Bring to a boil and cook until tender, about 10-15 minutes. Drain and let cool.
2. Hard boil the eggs: Place the eggs in a saucepan and cover with cold water. Bring to a boil, then remove from heat and let sit for 10 minutes. Peel and chop the eggs.
3. In a large bowl, combine the cooked potatoes, carrots, chopped eggs, diced ham or bologna, peas, pickles, and onion.
4. In a small bowl, mix together the mayonnaise and Dijon mustard. Pour over the salad and toss to coat.
5. Season with salt and pepper to taste. Refrigerate for at least 1 hour before serving.

Serving Suggestion: Serve chilled as a side dish or light lunch, garnished with fresh herbs if desired.

18. Ethiopian Doro Wat (Spicy Egg Stew):

- Preparation Time: 20 minutes
- Cooking Time: 1 hour 30 minutes
- Serves: 4-6

Ingredients:
- 6 large eggs

- 2 tablespoons vegetable oil
- 1 onion, finely chopped
- 3 cloves garlic, minced
- 1-inch piece ginger, grated
- 2 tablespoons berbere spice blend
- 1 teaspoon ground cumin
- 1 teaspoon ground coriander
- 1/2 teaspoon ground cardamom
- 1/4 teaspoon ground cloves
- 1 can (14 ounces) diced tomatoes
- 2 cups chicken broth
- Salt to taste
- Fresh cilantro, chopped, for garnish

Instructions:

1. Hard boil the eggs: Place the eggs in a saucepan and cover with cold water. Bring to a boil, then remove from heat and let sit for 10 minutes. Peel and set aside.

2. Heat the vegetable oil in a large pot over medium heat. Add the chopped onion and cook until softened, about 5 minutes.

3. Add the minced garlic, grated ginger, berbere spice blend, ground cumin, ground coriander, ground cardamom, and ground cloves to the pot. Cook for another 2 minutes, until fragrant.

4. Stir in the diced tomatoes and chicken broth. Bring the mixture to a simmer and cook for 20-30 minutes, until the sauce has thickened.

5. Gently add the peeled hard-boiled eggs to the pot and spoon some of the sauce over them. Simmer for another 20-30 minutes, stirring occasionally.

6. Season with salt to taste and garnish with chopped fresh cilantro before serving.

Serving Suggestion: Serve hot with injera (Ethiopian flatbread) or steamed rice for a traditional Ethiopian meal.

19. Vietnamese Egg Coffee:

- Preparation Time: 10 minutes
- Cooking Time: 5 minutes
- Serves: 1

Ingredients:
- 1 tablespoon finely ground Vietnamese coffee
- 2 tablespoons sweetened condensed milk
- 1 large egg
- Boiling water

Instructions:
1. Brew the Vietnamese coffee using a phin filter or a French press.
2. Pour the sweetened condensed milk into a heatproof glass.
3. Separate the egg yolk from the egg white and add the yolk to the glass with the sweetened condensed milk. Discard the egg white or save it for another use.
4. Whisk the egg yolk and sweetened condensed milk together until smooth and creamy.
5. Pour the brewed coffee into the glass, stirring gently to combine.
6. Serve immediately, optionally topped with a sprinkle of cocoa powder or cinnamon.

Serving Suggestion: Enjoy as a decadent and creamy dessert-like coffee drink.

20. Filipino Tortang Talong (Eggplant Omelette):

- Preparation Time: 15 minutes

- Cooking Time: 20 minutes
- Serves: 4

Ingredients:
- 4 large Asian eggplants
- 4 large eggs
- Salt and pepper to taste
- Vegetable oil for frying

Instructions:
1. Preheat the oven broiler or grill to high heat.
2. Pierce the eggplants in several places with a fork. Place them on a baking sheet and broil or grill, turning occasionally, until the skins are charred and the flesh is soft, about 10-15 minutes.
3. Remove the eggplants from the oven or grill and let them cool slightly. Peel off the charred skins and discard.
4. Flatten each eggplant with the back of a fork or spoon, spreading out the flesh.
5. In a bowl, beat the eggs and season with salt and pepper.
6. Heat a little vegetable oil in a large skillet over medium heat. Dip each flattened eggplant into the beaten eggs, coating both sides.
7. Carefully place the egg-coated eggplants in the skillet and fry until golden brown on both sides, about 2-3 minutes per side.
8. Remove the tortang along from the skillet and drain on paper towels. Serve hot.

Serving Suggestion: Serve with steamed rice and a dipping sauce made from vinegar, soy sauce, garlic, and chilli for a delicious and satisfying Filipino meal.

21. Malaysian Nasi Goreng Pattaya:

- Preparation Time: 20 minutes
- Cooking Time: 20 minutes
- Serves: 4

Ingredients:
- 4 cups cooked white rice, preferably day-old
- 2 tablespoons vegetable oil
- 1 onion, finely chopped
- 2 cloves garlic, minced
- 1 cup diced cooked chicken or shrimp
- 1 cup mixed vegetables (such as peas, carrots, and corn)
- 2 tablespoons soy sauce
- 2 tablespoons ketchup
- Salt and pepper to taste
- 4 large eggs
- Fresh cilantro, chopped, for garnish

Instructions:
1. Heat the vegetable oil in a large skillet or wok over medium heat. Add the chopped onion and minced garlic and cook until softened, about 5 minutes.
2. Add the diced chicken or shrimp to the skillet and cook until heated through, about 2-3 minutes.
3. Stir in the mixed vegetables and cook until tender, about 3-4 minutes.
4. Add the cooked white rice to the skillet and stir to combine.
5. Pour in the soy sauce and ketchup, stirring to evenly distribute.
6. Season with salt and pepper to taste.
7. Divide the fried rice mixture into 4 equal portions and shape each portion into a ball.

8. Heat a little more vegetable oil in the skillet over medium heat. Flatten each rice ball into a thin patty and cook until golden brown on both sides, about 2-3 minutes per side.

9. Remove the rice patties from the skillet and set aside.

10. In the same skillet, fry the eggs sunny-side up or over-easy.

11. To assemble, place a rice patty on each plate and top with a fried egg.

12. Garnish with chopped fresh cilantro before serving.

Serving Suggestion: Serve hot with a side of sliced cucumber and tomato for a complete Malaysian meal.

22. Brazilian Ovos Mexidos (Scrambled Eggs):

- Preparation Time: 5 minutes
- Cooking Time: 10 minutes
- Serves: 2

Ingredients:
- 4 large eggs
- 2 tablespoons milk
- Salt and pepper to taste
- 2 tablespoons butter
- 1/4 cup diced tomatoes
- 1/4 cup diced onions
- Fresh parsley, chopped, for garnish

Instructions:
1. In a bowl, whisk together the eggs, milk, salt, and pepper until well combined.

2. Heat the butter in a skillet over medium heat. Add the diced tomatoes and onions and cook until softened, about 3-4 minutes.

3. Pour the egg mixture into the skillet and cook, stirring gently, until the eggs are scrambled and cooked to your desired consistency.

4. Remove from heat and garnish with chopped fresh parsley before serving.

Serving Suggestion: Serve hot with toasted bread or as a filling for breakfast tacos.

23. Egyptian Feteer Meshaltet (Egyptian Pastry with Eggs):

- Preparation Time: 30 minutes
- Cooking Time: 15 minutes
- Serves: 4

Ingredients:
- 1 package of puff pastry dough
- 4 large eggs
- Salt and pepper to taste
- Butter or oil for brushing

Instructions:
1. Preheat the oven to 400°F (200°C). Line a baking sheet with parchment paper.

2. Roll out the puff pastry dough into a large rectangle.

3. Crack the eggs onto the centre of the pastry dough, leaving space between each egg.

4. Season the eggs with salt and pepper.

5. Fold the edges of the pastry dough over the eggs to create a border.

6. Brush the edges of the pastry dough with butter or oil.

7. Bake in the preheated oven for 12-15 minutes, or until the pastry is golden brown and the eggs are cooked to your desired doneness.

8. Serve hot, slicing the pastry into individual portions.

Serving Suggestion: Enjoy as a hearty breakfast or brunch dish with a side of salad or pickled vegetables.

24. Jamaican Ackee and Saltfish:

- Preparation Time: 20 minutes
- Cooking Time: 20 minutes
- Serves: 4

Ingredients:
- 1 can (19 ounces) ackee, drained and rinsed
- 1/2 pound salted codfish (saltfish), soaked overnight and flaked
- 2 tablespoons vegetable oil
- 1 onion, diced
- 1 bell pepper, diced
- 2 tomatoes, diced
- 2 cloves garlic, minced
- 2 scallions, chopped
- Scotch bonnet pepper or hot sauce to taste
- Salt and pepper to taste

Instructions:
1. Heat the vegetable oil in a skillet over medium heat. Add the diced onion, bell pepper, tomatoes, garlic, and scallions. Cook until softened, about 5-7 minutes.

2. Add the flaked saltfish to the skillet and cook for another 5 minutes, stirring occasionally.

3. Gently fold in the ackee and cook for an additional 5 minutes, being careful not to break up the ackee too much.

4. Season with Scotch bonnet pepper or hot sauce, salt, and pepper to taste.

5. Serve hot with fried dumplings, boiled green bananas, or breadfruit.

Serving Suggestion: Enjoy this traditional Jamaican dish as a flavorful breakfast or brunch option.

25. Iranian Nargesi Esfenaj (Spinach with Eggs):

- Preparation Time: 10 minutes
- Cooking Time: 15 minutes
- Serves: 4

Ingredients:
- 1 pound fresh spinach, washed and chopped
- 4 large eggs
- 2 tablespoons vegetable oil
- 1 onion, finely chopped
- 2 cloves garlic, minced
- 1 teaspoon ground turmeric
- Salt and pepper to taste
- Sumac for garnish (optional)

Instructions:
1. Heat the vegetable oil in a skillet over medium heat. Add the chopped onion and cook until softened, about 5 minutes.

2. Add the minced garlic and ground turmeric to the skillet and cook for another 2 minutes, until fragrant.

3. Add the chopped spinach to the skillet and cook until wilted, about 5-7 minutes.

4. Create small wells in the spinach mixture and crack an egg into each well.

5. Cover the skillet and cook for 5-7 minutes, until the egg whites are set but the yolks are still runny.

6. Season with salt and pepper to taste.

7. Garnish with a sprinkle of sumac before serving, if desired.

Serving Suggestion: Serve hot with flatbread or rice for a satisfying Iranian breakfast or brunch.

26. Belgian Liege Waffle with Egg:

- Preparation Time: 15 minutes
- Cooking Time: 5 minutes
- Serves: 1

Ingredients:
- 1 Belgian Liege waffle
- 1 large egg
- Butter or oil for frying
- Maple syrup or powdered sugar for serving

Instructions:

1. Preheat a skillet over medium heat and melt a little butter or add oil.

2. Crack the egg into the skillet and fry until the whites are set but the yolk is still runny.

3. While the egg is frying, warm the Belgian Liege waffle in a toaster or oven until heated through.

4. Place the fried egg on top of the warmed waffle.

5. Drizzle with maple syrup or sprinkle with powdered sugar before serving.

Serving Suggestion: Enjoy this indulgent breakfast or brunch dish with a side of fresh fruit or bacon.

27. Thai Khai Jiao (Stuffed Omelette):

- Preparation Time: 10 minutes
- Cooking Time: 10 minutes
- Serves: 2-4

Ingredients:
- 4 large eggs
- 1/2 cup ground pork or chicken
- 1/4 cup diced onion
- 1/4 cup diced tomatoes
- 2 tablespoons fish sauce
- 1 tablespoon soy sauce
- 1 tablespoon oyster sauce
- 1 tablespoon vegetable oil
- Fresh cilantro, chopped, for garnish

Instructions:
1. In a bowl, beat the eggs and set aside.
2. Heat the vegetable oil in a skillet over medium heat. Add the ground pork or chicken and cook until browned.
3. Add the diced onion and tomatoes to the skillet and cook until softened.
4. Pour the beaten eggs into the skillet, swirling to cover the bottom evenly.
5. Cook until the bottom is set and the edges are slightly golden.
6. Flip the omelette over and cook for another 1-2 minutes on the other side.
7. Remove from heat and transfer to a serving plate.
8. Garnish with chopped fresh cilantro before serving.

Serving Suggestion: Serve hot with steamed rice and a side of sweet chilli sauce for dipping.

28. South African Bobotie (Spiced Meat with Egg Custard):

- Preparation Time: 30 minutes
- Cooking Time: 1 hour
- Serves: 4-6

Ingredients:
- 1 pound ground beef or lamb
- 1 onion, finely chopped
- 2 cloves garlic, minced
- 2 tablespoons curry powder
- 1 teaspoon ground turmeric
- 1 teaspoon ground coriander
- 1 teaspoon ground cinnamon
- 1 tablespoon apricot jam
- 1 tablespoon lemon juice
- 1 cup milk
- 2 slices white bread, crusts removed
- 2 large eggs
- Salt and pepper to taste
- Bay leaves for garnish

Instructions:
1. Preheat the oven to 350°F (175°C). Grease a baking dish.
2. In a skillet, cook the ground meat, onion, and garlic over medium heat until the meat is browned and the onion is softened, about 8-10 minutes. Drain any excess fat.
3. Stir in the curry powder, turmeric, coriander, cinnamon, apricot jam, and lemon juice. Cook for another 2-3 minutes.

4. In a separate bowl, whisk together the milk and eggs. Tear the bread into small pieces and soak them in the milk mixture for a few minutes.

5. Add the soaked bread to the meat mixture and stir until well combined. Season with salt and pepper to taste.

6. Transfer the mixture to the prepared baking dish and smooth the top with a spatula. Arrange the bay leaves on top.

7. Bake in the preheated oven for 30-40 minutes, or until the custard is set and golden brown on top.

8. Serve hot with yellow rice and chutney.

Serving Suggestion: Garnish with chopped fresh cilantro or parsley before serving.

29. Spanish Huevos a la Flamenca:

- Preparation Time: 20 minutes
- Cooking Time: 30 minutes
- Serves: 4

Ingredients:
- 4 large eggs
- 1/2 cup diced chorizo sausage
- 1/2 cup diced serrano ham or bacon
- 1 onion, diced
- 2 cloves garlic, minced
- 1 red bell pepper, diced
- 1 green bell pepper, diced
- 1 can (14 ounces) diced tomatoes
- 1 teaspoon smoked paprika
- 1/2 teaspoon cayenne pepper (optional)
- Salt and pepper to taste
- Olive oil for cooking

- Fresh parsley, chopped, for garnish

Instructions:
1. Preheat the oven to 375°F (190°C).
2. Heat a little olive oil in a skillet over medium heat. Add the diced chorizo sausage and cook until browned.
3. Add the diced serrano ham or bacon to the skillet and cook until crispy.
4. Stir in the diced onion, garlic, and bell peppers. Cook until softened, about 5-7 minutes.
5. Add the diced tomatoes, smoked paprika, and cayenne pepper (if using). Simmer for another 5 minutes.
6. Using a spoon, make small wells in the tomato mixture and crack an egg into each well.
7. Transfer the skillet to the preheated oven and bake for 10-15 minutes, or until the eggs are cooked to your desired doneness.
8. Season with salt and pepper to taste and garnish with chopped fresh parsley before serving.

Serving Suggestion: Serve hot with crusty bread for dipping into the flavorful tomato sauce.

30. Italian Pasta Carbonara:
- Preparation Time: 10 minutes
- Cooking Time: 15 minutes
- Serves: 4

Ingredients:
- 12 ounces spaghetti or other long pasta
- 4 large eggs
- 1 cup grated Parmesan cheese, plus extra for serving
- 4 ounces pancetta or bacon, diced
- 2 cloves garlic, minced
- Salt and black pepper to taste

- Fresh parsley, chopped, for garnish

Instructions:
1. Cook the pasta according to package instructions until al dente. Reserve 1 cup of pasta cooking water, then drain the pasta and set aside.
2. In a bowl, whisk together the eggs and grated Parmesan cheese. Season with salt and black pepper.
3. In a skillet, cook the diced pancetta or bacon over medium heat until crispy. Add the minced garlic and cook for another minute.
4. Add the cooked pasta to the skillet with the pancetta and garlic. Remove from heat and quickly toss to combine.
5. Pour the egg and cheese mixture over the hot pasta, stirring quickly to coat the pasta evenly. Add reserved pasta cooking water as needed to create a creamy sauce.
6. Serve immediately, garnished with chopped fresh parsley and extra grated Parmesan cheese.

Serving Suggestion: Enjoy as a comforting and satisfying meal with a side salad and crusty bread.

31. French Quiche Lorraine:
- Preparation Time: 20 minutes
- Cooking Time: 40 minutes
- Serves: 6-8

Ingredients:
- 1 pie crust, homemade or store-bought
- 6 slices bacon, cooked and crumbled
- 1 onion, thinly sliced
- 1 cup grated Gruyere or Swiss cheese
- 4 large eggs
- 1 cup heavy cream
- Salt, pepper, and nutmeg to taste

Instructions:
1. Preheat the oven to 375°F (190°C).
2. Line a pie dish with the pie crust and crimp the edges.
3. Scatter the cooked and crumbled bacon, sliced onion, and grated cheese over the bottom of the pie crust.
4. In a bowl, whisk together the eggs, heavy cream, salt, pepper, and a pinch of nutmeg.
5. Pour the egg mixture over the bacon, onion, and cheese in the pie crust.
6. Bake in the preheated oven for 35-40 minutes, or until the quiche is set and the crust is golden brown.
7. Allow the quiche to cool for a few minutes before slicing and serving.

Serving Suggestion: Serve warm or at room temperature with a side of mixed greens dressed with vinaigrette.

32. Mexican Chilaquiles Verdes with Eggs:

- Preparation Time: 15 minutes
- Cooking Time: 20 minutes
- Serves: 4

Ingredients:
- 1 tablespoon vegetable oil
- 1 onion, thinly sliced
- 2 cloves garlic, minced
- 1 pound tomatillos, husks removed and quartered
- 1-2 jalapeno peppers, seeded and chopped
- 1 cup chicken broth
- Salt and pepper to taste
- 6 cups tortilla chips
- 4 large eggs

- Queso fresco or feta cheese, crumbled, for garnish
- Fresh cilantro, chopped, for garnish
- Lime wedges for serving

Instructions:
1. In a blender, combine the tomatillos, jalapeno peppers, and chicken broth. Blend until smooth.
2. Heat the vegetable oil in a large skillet over medium heat. Add the sliced onion and cook until softened, about 5 minutes.
3. Add the minced garlic to the skillet and cook for another minute.
4. Pour the blended tomatillo mixture into the skillet. Simmer for 10-15 minutes, stirring occasionally, until the sauce has thickened slightly. Season with salt and pepper to taste.
5. Add the tortilla chips to the skillet and toss to coat evenly in the sauce.
6. Make small wells in the tortilla chip mixture and crack an egg into each well.
7. Cover the skillet and cook for 5-7 minutes, or until the egg whites are set but the yolks are still runny.
8. Garnish with crumbled queso fresco or feta cheese and chopped fresh cilantro. Serve with lime wedges on the side.

Serving Suggestion: Enjoy hot as a hearty breakfast or brunch dish.

33. Lebanese Balila (Chickpeas with Eggs):

- Preparation Time: 10 minutes
- Cooking Time: 20 minutes
- Serves: 4

Ingredients:
- 2 tablespoons olive oil
- 1 onion, finely chopped
- 2 cloves garlic, minced
- 1 teaspoon ground cumin
- 1 teaspoon ground paprika
- 1/2 teaspoon ground turmeric
- 2 cans (15 ounces each) chickpeas, drained and rinsed
- 1 can (14 ounces) diced tomatoes
- 4 large eggs
- Salt and pepper to taste
- Fresh parsley, chopped, for garnish

Instructions:
1. Heat the olive oil in a skillet over medium heat. Add the chopped onion and cook until softened, about 5 minutes.
2. Add the minced garlic, ground cumin, ground paprika, and ground turmeric to the skillet. Cook for another 2 minutes, until fragrant.
3. Stir in the drained chickpeas and diced tomatoes. Simmer for 10-15 minutes, stirring occasionally.
4. Using a spoon, create small wells in the chickpea mixture and crack an egg into each well.
5. Cover the skillet and cook for 5-7 minutes, until the egg whites are set but the yolks are still runny.
6. Season with salt and pepper to taste.
7. Garnish with chopped fresh parsley before serving.

Serving Suggestion: Serve hot with warm pita bread or Lebanese flatbread for a satisfying meal.

34. Indian Egg Biryani:
- Preparation Time: 30 minutes
- Cooking Time: 45 minutes
- Serves: 4

Ingredients:
- 2 cups basmati rice, rinsed and soaked for 30 minutes
- 4 hard-boiled eggs, peeled and halved
- 2 onions, thinly sliced
- 2 tomatoes, chopped
- 1/2 cup plain yoghourt
- 1/4 cup chopped fresh cilantro
- 1/4 cup chopped fresh mint
- 1/4 cup fried onions (optional, for garnish)
- 2 tablespoons ghee or vegetable oil
- 1 tablespoon ginger-garlic paste
- 1 teaspoon cumin seeds
- 1 teaspoon ground coriander
- 1 teaspoon ground turmeric
- 1 teaspoon garam masala
- Salt to taste

Instructions:
1. Heat ghee or oil in a large skillet over medium heat. Add cumin seeds and let them splutter.
2. Add sliced onions and sauté until golden brown.
3. Stir in ginger-garlic paste and cook until fragrant.
4. Add chopped tomatoes, ground coriander, ground turmeric, and salt. Cook until tomatoes are softened.
5. Add yoghurt and cook for 2-3 minutes.
6. Layer half of the cooked rice in a deep pot. Top with half of the egg halves and half of the tomato-yoghourt mixture.
7. Repeat the layers with the remaining rice, eggs, and tomato-yoghourt mixture.
8. Sprinkle garam masala, chopped cilantro, and mint over the top layer.
9. Cover the pot and cook on low heat for 15-20 minutes, until the flavours are well combined and the rice is cooked through.

10. Garnish with fried onions before serving.

Serving Suggestion: Serve hot with raita (yoghourt sauce) and cucumber-tomato salad.

35. Moroccan B'stilla (Savoury Pie with Eggs):

- Preparation Time: 45 minutes
- Cooking Time: 1 hour
- Serves: 6-8

Ingredients:
- 8 sheets phyllo pastry
- 4 tablespoons unsalted butter, melted
- 1 onion, finely chopped
- 2 cloves garlic, minced
- 1 teaspoon ground ginger
- 1 teaspoon ground cinnamon
- 1/2 teaspoon ground turmeric
- 1/2 teaspoon ground nutmeg
- 1/4 teaspoon ground cloves
- 1/4 teaspoon ground black pepper
- 2 cups cooked shredded chicken
- 1/2 cup blanched almonds, toasted and chopped
- 1/4 cup chopped fresh parsley
- 4 large eggs, beaten
- Powdered sugar for dusting

Instructions:
1. Preheat the oven to 375°F (190°C). Grease a pie dish with butter.
2. In a skillet, heat a tablespoon of butter over medium heat. Add chopped onion and garlic and cook until softened.

3. Stir in ground ginger, ground cinnamon, ground turmeric, ground nutmeg, ground cloves, and ground black pepper. Cook for 1-2 minutes.

4. Add cooked shredded chicken, chopped almonds, and chopped parsley. Cook for another 2-3 minutes.

5. Spread half of the phyllo pastry sheets in the prepared pie dish, brushing each sheet with melted butter.

6. Spread the chicken mixture evenly over the phyllo pastry.

7. Pour beaten eggs over the chicken mixture.

8. Top with the remaining phyllo pastry sheets, brushing each sheet with melted butter.

9. Tuck the edges of the pastry into the dish to seal the pie.

10. Bake in the preheated oven for 30-35 minutes, or until the pastry is golden brown and crispy.

11. Remove from the oven and let cool for a few minutes before dusting with powdered sugar.

12. Slice and serve warm.

Serving Suggestion: Serve as a main dish with a side of Moroccan salad or couscous.

36. Chinese Tea Eggs (Marbled Eggs):

- Preparation Time: 10 minutes
- Cooking Time: 1 hour 30 minutes
- Serves: 6

Ingredients:
- 6 large eggs
- 2 tablespoons black tea leaves
- 2 star anise
- 2 cinnamon sticks

- 2 tablespoons soy sauce
- 1 teaspoon sugar
- Water for boiling

Instructions:
1. Place the eggs in a pot and cover with cold water. Bring to a boil over high heat.
2. Once boiling, reduce the heat to low and simmer for 5 minutes.
3. Remove the eggs from the pot and let them cool slightly.
4. Use the back of a spoon to gently tap the eggs all over, cracking the shells without peeling them.
5. In a separate pot, combine black tea leaves, star anise, cinnamon sticks, soy sauce, sugar, and enough water to cover the eggs.
6. Add the cracked eggs to the tea mixture and bring to a boil.
7. Reduce the heat to low and simmer for 1-2 hours, adding more water if needed to keep the eggs submerged.
8. Remove the pot from the heat and let the eggs cool in the tea mixture.
9. Once cooled, remove the eggs from the tea mixture and peel off the shells.
10. Slice the tea eggs in half and serve.

Serving Suggestion: Enjoy as a snack or appetiser with a sprinkle of salt and pepper.

37. Turkish Cilbir (Poached Eggs in Yogurt):
- Preparation Time: 10 minutes
- Cooking Time: 10 minutes
- Serves: 2

Ingredients:
- 4 large eggs
- 2 cups plain yoghourt
- 2 cloves garlic, minced
- 2 tablespoons butter
- 1 teaspoon paprika
- Salt and pepper to taste
- Fresh parsley, chopped, for garnish
- Turkish bread or crusty bread for serving

Instructions:
1. Fill a large saucepan with water and bring to a gentle simmer over medium heat.
2. Crack the eggs into separate small bowls or cups.
3. Carefully slide the eggs into the simmering water and poach for 3-4 minutes, until the whites are set but the yolks are still runny.
4. While the eggs are poaching, mix the plain yoghurt with minced garlic and season with salt and pepper.
5. Divide the garlic yoghourt between two serving plates, spreading it out into a thin layer.
6. Once the eggs are poached, use a slotted spoon to remove them from the water and place them on top of the garlic yoghourt.
7. In a small saucepan, melt the butter over low heat. Add paprika and cook for 1-2 minutes, until fragrant.
8. Drizzle the paprika butter over the poached eggs and yoghourt.
9. Garnish with chopped fresh parsley before serving.
10. Serve immediately with Turkish bread or crusty bread for dipping.

Serving Suggestion: Enjoy as a hearty breakfast or brunch dish.

38. Nigerian Egg Stew:

- Preparation Time: 15 minutes
- Cooking Time: 30 minutes
- Serves: 4

Ingredients:
- 4 large eggs
- 4 ripe tomatoes, blended into a puree
- 1 onion, finely chopped
- 2 bell peppers (red and green), finely chopped
- 2 cloves garlic, minced
- 1 teaspoon ground paprika
- 1/2 teaspoon ground cayenne pepper (optional)
- 2 tablespoons vegetable oil
- Salt and pepper to taste
- Fresh cilantro or parsley, chopped, for garnish

Instructions:
1. Hard-boil the eggs, peel them, and set aside.
2. Heat vegetable oil in a large skillet over medium heat. Add chopped onion and cook until softened.
3. Add minced garlic and cook for another minute.
4. Stir in blended tomatoes, chopped bell peppers, ground paprika, and ground cayenne pepper (if using). Cook for 15-20 minutes, stirring occasionally, until the stew thickens.
5. Carefully add the hard-boiled eggs to the stew, spooning some of the stew over the eggs to coat them.

6. Simmer for another 5-10 minutes to allow the flavours to meld together.
   7. Season with salt and pepper to taste.
   8. Garnish with chopped fresh cilantro or parsley before serving.

   Serving Suggestion: Enjoy with boiled yams, plantains, or rice.

39. Cuban Huevos Habaneros:

- Preparation Time: 10 minutes
- Cooking Time: 15 minutes
- Serves: 2

Ingredients:
- 4 large eggs
- 1 onion, thinly sliced
- 1 bell pepper, thinly sliced
- 2 cloves garlic, minced
- 1 tomato, chopped
- 1 tablespoon olive oil
- 1/2 teaspoon ground cumin
- 1/2 teaspoon dried oregano
- Salt and pepper to taste
- Fresh cilantro, chopped, for garnish

Instructions:
   1. Heat olive oil in a skillet over medium heat. Add sliced onion and bell pepper and cook until softened.
   2. Add minced garlic, ground cumin, and dried oregano to the skillet. Cook for another minute, until fragrant.
   3. Stir in chopped tomato and cook until softened and slightly thickened.
   4. Crack the eggs into the skillet, spacing them evenly among the vegetables.

5. Cover the skillet and cook for 5-7 minutes, until the eggs are cooked to your desired doneness.

6. Season with salt and pepper to taste.

7. Garnish with chopped fresh cilantro before serving.

Serving Suggestion: Serve hot with crusty bread or warm tortillas for a delicious Cuban breakfast or brunch.

40. Thai Khai Yad Sai (Stuffed Eggs):

- Preparation Time: 20 minutes
- Cooking Time: 20 minutes
- Serves: 4

Ingredients:
- 6 hard-boiled eggs, peeled
- 1/2 cup ground pork or chicken
- 1/4 cup finely chopped onion
- 1/4 cup finely chopped tomatoes
- 2 tablespoons fish sauce
- 1 tablespoon soy sauce
- 1 tablespoon oyster sauce
- 1 tablespoon vegetable oil
- 1 teaspoon sugar
- 1/2 teaspoon ground black pepper
- Fresh cilantro, chopped, for garnish

Instructions:

1. Cut the hard-boiled eggs in half lengthwise and carefully remove the yolks.

2. In a bowl, mash the egg yolks with a fork and set aside.

3. Heat vegetable oil in a skillet over medium heat. Add ground pork or chicken and cook until browned.

4. Add chopped onion and tomatoes to the skillet and cook until softened.

5. Stir in fish sauce, soy sauce, oyster sauce, sugar, and ground black pepper. Cook for another 2-3 minutes.

6. Fill each egg white half with the meat mixture.

7. Spoon the mashed egg yolk mixture on top of the meat mixture in each egg white half.

8. Place the stuffed eggs on a serving platter and garnish with chopped fresh cilantro before serving.

Serving Suggestion: Serve hot as an appetiser or side dish with steamed rice.

41. Australian Avocado Toast with Poached Egg:

- Preparation Time: 10 minutes
- Cooking Time: 5 minutes
- Serves: 2

Ingredients:
- 2 slices whole-grain bread, toasted
- 1 ripe avocado, mashed
- 2 large eggs
- 1 tablespoon white vinegar
- Salt and pepper to taste
- Red pepper flakes for garnish (optional)
- Lemon wedges for serving

Instructions:

1. Spread mashed avocado evenly onto the toasted whole-grain bread slices.
2. Fill a medium saucepan with water and bring it to a gentle simmer over medium heat.
3. Add white vinegar to the simmering water.
4. Crack one egg into a small bowl or cup.
5. Carefully slide the egg into the simmering water. Repeat with the second egg.
6. Poach the eggs for 3-4 minutes, until the whites are set but the yolks are still runny.
7. Use a slotted spoon to remove the poached eggs from the water and drain excess water on a paper towel.
8. Place one poached egg on top of each avocado toast.
9. Season with salt, pepper, and red pepper flakes (if using).
10. Serve immediately with lemon wedges on the side.

Serving Suggestion: Enjoy as a nutritious breakfast or brunch option.

42. Japanese Onsen Tamago (Soft-Boiled Eggs):

- Preparation Time: 1 minute
- Cooking Time: 45 minutes
- Serves: 2

Ingredients:
- 2 large eggs
- Warm water

Instructions:
1. Fill a large bowl with warm water.
2. Place the eggs in the warm water and cover the bowl.
3. Let the eggs sit in the warm water for 45 minutes.

4. After 45 minutes, carefully crack the eggs open and remove them from the shells.

5. Serve immediately as a topping for rice or noodles, or use in other dishes.

Serving Suggestion: Enjoy as a traditional Japanese breakfast or as a topping for ramen or udon noodles.

43. Korean Bibimbap with Fried Egg:

- Preparation Time: 30 minutes
- Cooking Time: 30 minutes
- Serves: 4

Ingredients:
- 2 cups cooked short-grain rice
- 1 cup cooked bulgogi beef or tofu
- 1 cup julienned carrots, sautéed
- 1 cup julienned zucchini, sautéed
- 1 cup spinach, blanched and seasoned with sesame oil
- 4 large eggs
- 4 tablespoons gochujang (Korean red pepper paste)
- 2 tablespoons sesame oil
- 2 tablespoons vegetable oil
- Salt and pepper to taste
- Sesame seeds for garnish
- Kimchi for serving (optional)

Instructions:
1. Divide the cooked rice among serving bowls.
2. Arrange the bulgogi beef or tofu, sautéed carrots, sautéed zucchini, and seasoned spinach on top of the rice in each bowl.

3. Heat vegetable oil in a skillet over medium heat. Crack an egg into the skillet and fry until the whites are set but the yolk is still runny. Repeat with the remaining eggs.

4. Place a fried egg on top of each bibimbap bowl.

5. Drizzle sesame oil and gochujang over each bowl.

6. Sprinkle with sesame seeds and season with salt and pepper to taste.

7. Serve hot with kimchi on the side, if desired.

Serving Suggestion: Mix everything together before eating to enjoy all the flavours combined.

44. Egyptian Koshari with Fried Egg:

- Preparation Time: 30 minutes
- Cooking Time: 45 minutes
- Serves: 4

Ingredients:
- 2 cups cooked rice
- 1 cup cooked lentils
- 1 cup cooked macaroni
- 1 cup cooked chickpeas
- 1 onion, thinly sliced and fried until crispy
- 4 large eggs
- 4 tablespoons vegetable oil
- Salt and pepper to taste
- Tomato sauce for serving

Instructions:

1. Divide the cooked rice, lentils, macaroni, and chickpeas among serving plates.

2. Heat vegetable oil in a skillet over medium heat. Crack an egg into the skillet and fry until the whites are set but the yolk is still runny. Repeat with the remaining eggs.

3. Place a fried egg on top of each serving plate.

4. Sprinkle fried onion over each plate.

5. Season with salt and pepper to taste.

6. Serve hot with tomato sauce on the side.

Serving Suggestion: Mix everything together before eating to enjoy all the flavours combined.

45. Brazilian Pão de Queijo with Egg:

- Preparation Time: 15 minutes
- Cooking Time: 25 minutes
- Serves: 4

Ingredients:

- 1 cup tapioca flour
- 1/2 cup milk
- 1/4 cup vegetable oil
- 1/2 cup grated Parmesan cheese
- 1/2 teaspoon salt
- 2 large eggs
- Butter for greasing

Instructions:

1. Preheat the oven to 375°F (190°C). Grease a mini muffin tin with butter.

2. In a saucepan, combine milk and vegetable oil and heat until just before boiling.

3. In a mixing bowl, combine tapioca flour, grated Parmesan cheese, and salt.

4. Pour the hot milk mixture over the tapioca flour mixture and stir until well combined.

5. Allow the mixture to cool slightly, then beat in the eggs one at a time until smooth.

6. Fill each mini muffin cup with the batter.

7. Bake in the preheated oven for 20-25 minutes, or until puffed up and golden brown.

8. Remove from the oven and let cool for a few minutes before serving.

Serving Suggestion: Enjoy warm as a delicious breakfast or snack with a cup of coffee or tea.

46. Mexican Migas:

- Preparation Time: 10 minutes
- Cooking Time: 15 minutes
- Serves: 4

Ingredients:
- 4 large eggs
- 4 corn tortillas, cut into strips
- 1/2 onion, chopped
- 1 jalapeño pepper, seeded and diced
- 2 tomatoes, diced
- 1/2 cup shredded cheddar cheese
- 2 tablespoons vegetable oil
- Salt and pepper to taste
- Fresh cilantro, chopped, for garnish
- Lime wedges for serving

Instructions:

1. Heat vegetable oil in a large skillet over medium heat.

2. Add chopped onion and diced jalapeño pepper to the skillet. Cook until softened.

3. Stir in corn tortilla strips and cook until slightly crispy.

4. Add diced tomatoes to the skillet and cook for another 2-3 minutes.

5. Crack the eggs directly into the skillet and scramble them with the tortilla mixture until cooked through.

6. Sprinkle shredded cheddar cheese over the migas and cook until melted.

7. Season with salt and pepper to taste.

8. Garnish with chopped fresh cilantro and serve with lime wedges on the side.

Serving Suggestion: Enjoy hot with refried beans and avocado slices.

47. Italian Eggplant Parmesan:

- Preparation Time: 30 minutes
- Cooking Time: 1 hour
- Serves: 6

Ingredients:
- 2 large eggplants, sliced into rounds
- 2 cups marinara sauce
- 2 cups shredded mozzarella cheese
- 1/2 cup grated Parmesan cheese
- 1 cup all-purpose flour
- 2 large eggs, beaten
- 1 cup breadcrumbs
- 2 tablespoons olive oil
- Salt and pepper to taste
- Fresh basil leaves for garnish

Instructions:

1. Preheat the oven to 375°F (190°C). Grease a baking dish with olive oil.

2. Season eggplant slices with salt and pepper. Dip each slice into flour, then beaten eggs, and finally breadcrumbs, coating evenly.

3. Arrange the breaded eggplant slices in the prepared baking dish. Bake for 20-25 minutes, until golden brown and crispy.

4. Remove the baking dish from the oven. Spread marinara sauce over the eggplant slices.

5. Sprinkle shredded mozzarella cheese and grated Parmesan cheese over the marinara sauce.

6. Return the baking dish to the oven and bake for another 20-25 minutes, until the cheese is melted and bubbly.

7. Garnish with fresh basil leaves before serving.

Serving Suggestion: Serve hot with a side of spaghetti or garlic bread.

48. Greek Avgolemono Soup:

- Preparation Time: 10 minutes
- Cooking Time: 30 minutes
- Serves: 4

Ingredients:
- 6 cups chicken broth
- 1/2 cup orzo pasta
- 3 eggs
- Juice of 2 lemons
- Salt and pepper to taste
- Fresh dill, chopped, for garnish

Instructions:

1. In a large pot, bring chicken broth to a boil over medium heat.

2. Add orzo pasta to the boiling broth and cook until tender, about 10 minutes.

3. In a mixing bowl, whisk together eggs and lemon juice until well combined.

4. Slowly add a ladleful of hot broth to the egg mixture, whisking constantly to temper the eggs.

5. Gradually pour the egg mixture back into the pot, stirring constantly.

6. Cook for another 5-10 minutes, stirring occasionally, until the soup thickens slightly.

7. Season with salt and pepper to taste.

8. Garnish with chopped fresh dill before serving.

Serving Suggestion: Enjoy hot as a comforting and tangy soup.

49. Turkish Manti with Yogurt and Egg:

- Preparation Time: 1 hour
- Cooking Time: 30 minutes
- Serves: 4

Ingredients:

- 1 package (500g) store-bought manti (Turkish dumplings)
- 2 cups plain yoghourt
- 2 cloves garlic, minced
- 2 tablespoons butter
- 1 teaspoon paprika
- Salt and pepper to taste
- Fresh parsley, chopped, for garnish

Instructions:

1. Cook manti according to package instructions until tender. Drain and set aside.

2. In a bowl, mix plain yoghourt with minced garlic and season with salt to taste.

3. Heat butter in a skillet over medium heat. Add paprika and cook for 1-2 minutes, until fragrant.

4. Add cooked manti to the skillet and toss to coat evenly in the butter mixture.

5. Divide the manti among serving plates.

6. Spoon garlic yoghourt over the manti.

7. Top each plate with a fried egg.

8. Garnish with chopped fresh parsley before serving.

Serving Suggestion: Serve hot with a sprinkle of red pepper flakes and a side of Turkish bread.

50. Spanish Migas with Chorizo and Egg:

- Preparation Time: 15 minutes
- Cooking Time: 20 minutes
- Serves: 4

Ingredients:
- 4 large eggs
- 4 slices stale bread, torn into small pieces
- 100g chorizo sausage, diced
- 1 onion, chopped
- 2 cloves garlic, minced
- 1 red bell pepper, diced
- 1 green bell pepper, diced

- 2 tablespoons olive oil
- Salt and pepper to taste
- Fresh parsley, chopped, for garnish

Instructions:
1. Heat olive oil in a large skillet over medium heat. Add diced chorizo and cook until slightly crispy.
2. Add chopped onion and minced garlic to the skillet. Cook until softened.
3. Stir in diced bell peppers and cook until tender.
4. Add torn bread pieces to the skillet and toss to coat evenly in the chorizo and vegetable mixture.
5. Cook for another 10-15 minutes, stirring occasionally, until the bread is crispy and golden brown.
6. Meanwhile, heat a separate skillet over medium heat. Crack an egg into the skillet and fry until the whites are set but the yolk is still runny. Repeat with the remaining eggs.
7. Divide the migas among serving plates.
8. Top each plate with a fried egg.
9. Season with salt and pepper to taste.
10. Garnish with chopped fresh parsley before serving.

Serving Suggestion: Serve hot with a side of roasted vegetables or a simple salad.

51. Thai Khai Jiao Khanom Pang (Egg Toast):

- Preparation Time: 10 minutes
- Cooking Time: 10 minutes
- Serves: 4

Ingredients:
- 8 slices sandwich bread
- 4 large eggs

- 1/4 cup condensed milk
- 2 tablespoons vegetable oil
- Butter for spreading
- Sugar for sprinkling

Instructions:
1. In a shallow bowl, whisk together eggs and condensed milk until well combined.
2. Heat vegetable oil in a skillet over medium heat.
3. Dip each slice of bread into the egg mixture, ensuring it is well coated on both sides.
4. Place the dipped bread slices in the skillet and cook until golden brown and crispy on both sides.
5. Remove from the skillet and spread butter on each toast.
6. Sprinkle sugar over the buttered toasts.
7. Serve hot as a sweet and savoury breakfast or snack.

Serving Suggestion: Enjoy with a cup of Thai milk tea or coffee for a delicious and satisfying treat.

52. Moroccan Mealmen with Egg:

- Preparation Time: 15 minutes
- Cooking Time: 30 minutes
- Serves: 4

Ingredients:
- 4 large eggs
- 2 cups cooked couscous
- 1 onion, finely chopped
- 2 tomatoes, diced
- 1 bell pepper, diced
- 2 cloves garlic, minced
- 1 teaspoon ground cumin

- 1 teaspoon ground paprika
- 1/2 teaspoon ground cinnamon
- 1/4 teaspoon ground turmeric
- 2 tablespoons olive oil
- Salt and pepper to taste
- Fresh cilantro, chopped, for garnish

Instructions:
1. Heat olive oil in a skillet over medium heat. Add chopped onion and minced garlic. Cook until softened.
2. Add diced tomatoes and diced bell pepper to the skillet. Cook until softened.
3. Stir in ground cumin, ground paprika, ground cinnamon, and ground turmeric. Cook for another 2-3 minutes.
4. Add cooked couscous to the skillet and toss to coat evenly in the vegetable and spice mixture.
5. Create four wells in the couscous mixture and crack an egg into each well.
6. Cover the skillet and cook for 8-10 minutes, until the eggs are cooked to your desired doneness.
7. Season with salt and pepper to taste.
8. Garnish with chopped fresh cilantro before serving.

Serving Suggestion: Serve hot as a main dish or side dish with crusty bread.

53. Nigerian Egg Roll:

- Preparation Time: 20 minutes
- Cooking Time: 20 minutes
- Serves: 6

Ingredients:
- 6 hard-boiled eggs
- 2 cups all-purpose flour
- 1/2 cup sugar

- 1/4 cup butter, melted
- 1 teaspoon baking powder
- 1/2 teaspoon salt
- 1/2 cup milk
- Vegetable oil for frying

Instructions:
1. In a mixing bowl, combine all-purpose flour, sugar, baking powder, and salt.
2. Gradually add melted butter and milk to the dry ingredients, mixing until a smooth dough forms.
3. Divide the dough into 6 equal portions.
4. Flatten each portion of dough into a circle and wrap it around a hard-boiled egg, ensuring the egg is completely covered.
5. Heat vegetable oil in a deep fryer or skillet over medium heat.
6. Fry the egg rolls in the hot oil until golden brown and crispy on all sides.
7. Remove from the oil and drain on paper towels.
8. Serve hot or at room temperature.

Serving Suggestion: Enjoy as a snack or appetiser with a dipping sauce of your choice.

54. Indonesian Nasi Goreng with Egg:

- Preparation Time: 20 minutes
- Cooking Time: 15 minutes
- Serves: 4

Ingredients:
- 4 cups cooked rice, preferably cold
- 2 chicken breasts, cooked and shredded

- 2 eggs
- 1 onion, chopped
- 2 cloves garlic, minced
- 2 tablespoons soy sauce
- 1 tablespoon kecap manis (sweet soy sauce)
- 1 teaspoon ground coriander
- 1 teaspoon ground cumin
- 1/2 teaspoon ground turmeric
- 2 tablespoons vegetable oil
- Salt and pepper to taste
- Fresh cilantro, chopped, for garnish
- Fried shallots for garnish (optional)

Instructions:

1. Heat vegetable oil in a large skillet or wok over medium heat. Add chopped onion and minced garlic. Cook until softened.

2. Add shredded chicken to the skillet and cook until heated through.

3. Push the chicken mixture to one side of the skillet and crack the eggs into the other side. Scramble the eggs until cooked through.

4. Stir in cooked rice, soy sauce, kecap manis, ground coriander, ground cumin, and ground turmeric. Cook until heated through and well combined.

5. Season with salt and pepper to taste.

6. Garnish with chopped fresh cilantro and fried shallots before serving.

Serving Suggestion: Serve hot with prawn crackers and a side of sliced cucumbers and tomatoes.

55. Brazilian Coxinha de Galinha (Chicken Croquette with Egg):

- Preparation Time: 40 minutes
- Cooking Time: 20 minutes
- Serves: 6

Ingredients:
- 2 cups shredded cooked chicken
- 2 cups chicken broth
- 1 onion, chopped
- 2 cloves garlic, minced
- 2 tablespoons vegetable oil
- 2 cups all-purpose flour
- 2 cups water
- 2 eggs
- Bread crumbs for coating
- Salt and pepper to taste
- Vegetable oil for frying

Instructions:
1. Heat vegetable oil in a skillet over medium heat. Add chopped onion and minced garlic. Cook until softened.
2. Add shredded cooked chicken to the skillet and cook until heated through. Season with salt and pepper to taste.
3. In a separate saucepan, bring chicken broth to a boil. Gradually add all-purpose flour to the boiling broth, stirring constantly, until a thick dough forms.
4. Remove the dough from the heat and let it cool slightly.
5. Take a small portion of the dough and flatten it in the palm of your hand. Place a spoonful of the chicken mixture in the centre of the dough and shape it into a croquette.
6. Beat the eggs in a shallow bowl. Dip each croquette into the beaten eggs, then coat evenly in bread crumbs.
7. Heat vegetable oil in a deep fryer or skillet over medium heat. Fry the croquettes in the hot oil until golden brown and crispy.
8. Remove from the oil and drain on paper towels.
9. Serve hot as a snack or appetiser.

56. Lebanese Fatteh with Egg:

- Preparation Time: 15 minutes
- Cooking Time: 30 minutes
- Serves: 4

Ingredients:
- 4 large eggs
- 2 cups cooked chickpeas
- 2 cups plain yoghourt
- 2 cloves garlic, minced
- 2 tablespoons tahini
- 2 tablespoons lemon juice
- 2 cups stale pita bread, torn into small pieces
- 2 tablespoons butter
- 1 teaspoon ground cumin
- Salt and pepper to taste
- Fresh parsley, chopped, for garnish

Instructions:
1. Preheat the oven to 350°F (175°C).
2. Spread torn pita bread pieces on a baking sheet and toast in the preheated oven for 10-15 minutes, until crispy.
3. In a mixing bowl, combine plain yoghourt with minced garlic, tahini, and lemon juice. Season with salt to taste.
4. In a skillet, melt butter over medium heat. Add cooked chickpeas and ground cumin. Cook until heated through.
5. Poach the eggs in simmering water until the whites are set but the yolks are still runny.
6. To assemble, spread toasted pita bread pieces on a serving platter. Top with cooked chickpeas.
7. Spoon garlic yoghourt mixture over the chickpeas.

8. Place poached eggs on top of the yoghourt mixture.
9. Garnish with chopped fresh parsley before serving.

Serving Suggestion: Serve hot as a hearty breakfast or brunch dish.

57. Italian Eggplant Involtini:

- Preparation Time: 30 minutes
- Cooking Time: 40 minutes
- Serves: 4

Ingredients:
- 2 large eggplants, sliced lengthwise
- 1 cup ricotta cheese
- 1/2 cup grated Parmesan cheese
- 1/4 cup chopped fresh basil
- 2 cloves garlic, minced
- 1 egg
- 2 cups marinara sauce
- Salt and pepper to taste
- Olive oil for drizzling

Instructions:
1. Preheat the oven to 375°F (190°C). Grease a baking dish with olive oil.
2. Place eggplant slices on a baking sheet. Drizzle with olive oil and season with salt and pepper. Roast in the preheated oven for 15-20 minutes, until tender.
3. In a mixing bowl, combine ricotta cheese, grated Parmesan cheese, chopped fresh basil, minced garlic, and egg. Season with salt and pepper to taste.
4. Spread a spoonful of marinara sauce on each eggplant slice.
5. Place a dollop of the ricotta mixture at one end of each eggplant slice and roll it up tightly.

6. Place the rolled eggplant slices seam-side down in the prepared baking dish.

7. Spoon marinara sauce over the eggplant involtini.

8. Bake in the preheated oven for 20-25 minutes, until heated through and bubbly.

9. Serve hot, garnished with additional grated Parmesan cheese and fresh basil.

Serving Suggestion: Enjoy as a delicious appetiser or main dish with a side of garlic bread or salad.

58. Korean Japchae with Egg:

- Preparation Time: 30 minutes
- Cooking Time: 20 minutes
- Serves: 4

Ingredients:
- 4 large eggs
- 200g sweet potato noodles (dangmyeon)
- 1 carrot, julienned
- 1 onion, thinly sliced
- 1 red bell pepper, thinly sliced
- 100g spinach
- 3 tablespoons soy sauce
- 2 tablespoons sesame oil
- 2 tablespoons brown sugar
- 2 cloves garlic, minced
- Vegetable oil for stir-frying
- Toasted sesame seeds for garnish

Instructions:
1. Cook sweet potato noodles according to package instructions. Drain and set aside.

2. Blanch spinach in boiling water for 30 seconds, then rinse with cold water and squeeze out excess moisture. Cut into smaller pieces.

3. Heat vegetable oil in a large skillet over medium heat. Add sliced onion and stir-fry until translucent.

4. Add julienned carrot and red bell pepper to the skillet. Stir-fry until tender-crisp.

5. Push the vegetables to one side of the skillet and crack the eggs into the other side. Scramble until cooked through.

6. Add cooked sweet potato noodles and blanched spinach to the skillet.

7. In a small bowl, mix soy sauce, sesame oil, brown sugar, and minced garlic. Pour over the noodle mixture.

8. Stir-fry everything together until well combined and heated through.

9. Garnish with toasted sesame seeds before serving.

Serving Suggestion: Serve hot as a main dish or side dish with a bowl of steamed rice.

59. Mexican Tacos de Papa con Huevo (Potato and Egg Tacos):

- Preparation Time: 20 minutes
- Cooking Time: 20 minutes
- Serves: 4

Ingredients:

- 8 small corn tortillas
- 4 large eggs
- 2 medium potatoes, peeled and diced
- 1/2 onion, diced
- 1 jalapeño pepper, seeded and diced
- 2 cloves garlic, minced
- 1/2 teaspoon ground cumin
- 1/2 teaspoon chilli powder
- Salt and pepper to taste
- Vegetable oil for frying
- Salsa, avocado slices, and cilantro for serving

Instructions:
1. Heat vegetable oil in a skillet over medium heat. Add diced potatoes and cook until golden brown and crispy. Remove from the skillet and drain on paper towels.
2. In the same skillet, add diced onion and jalapeño pepper. Cook until softened.
3. Add minced garlic, ground cumin, and chilli powder to the skillet. Cook for another minute.
4. Return the cooked potatoes to the skillet and toss to combine with the onion mixture.
5. Push the potato mixture to one side of the skillet and crack the eggs into the other side. Scramble until cooked through.
6. Warm corn tortillas in a dry skillet or microwave.
7. Spoon some of the potato and egg mixture onto each warm tortilla.
8. Top with salsa, avocado slices, and cilantro before serving.

Serving Suggestion: Serve hot with a squeeze of lime juice and a side of refried beans.

60. Chinese Century Egg Congee:

- Preparation Time: 10 minutes
- Cooking Time: 1 hour
- Serves: 4

Ingredients:
- 1 cup rice, rinsed
- 6 cups chicken broth
- 2 century eggs, peeled and diced
- 2 tablespoons minced ginger
- Salt and white pepper to taste
- Green onions, thinly sliced, for garnish
- Fried shallots for garnish
- Soy sauce for serving

Instructions:
1. In a large pot, bring chicken broth to a boil over medium heat.
2. Add rinsed rice to the boiling broth. Reduce heat to low and simmer, stirring occasionally, until the rice is cooked and the congee thickens, about 1 hour.
3. Stir in diced century eggs and minced ginger. Cook for another 5 minutes.
4. Season with salt and white pepper to taste.
5. Ladle the congee into serving bowls.
6. Garnish with thinly sliced green onions and fried shallots.
7. Serve hot with soy sauce on the side.

Serving Suggestion: Enjoy as a comforting breakfast or light meal.

61. Thai Kai Look Kuey (Son-in-Law Eggs):

- Preparation Time: 20 minutes

- Cooking Time: 20 minutes
- Serves: 4

Ingredients:
- 8 large eggs
- Vegetable oil for frying
- 1/2 cup tamarind paste
- 1/4 cup palm sugar
- 2 tablespoons fish sauce
- 2 shallots, thinly sliced
- 2 tablespoons roasted peanuts, chopped
- Fresh cilantro leaves for garnish
- Red chilli slices for garnish

Instructions:
1. Place eggs in a saucepan and cover with cold water. Bring to a boil over medium-high heat. Reduce heat to low and simmer for 7 minutes.
2. Transfer boiled eggs to a bowl of ice water and let cool completely. Peel the eggs and pat dry with paper towels.
3. Heat vegetable oil in a deep fryer or skillet over medium heat. Fry the peeled eggs until golden brown and crispy. Remove from the oil and drain on paper towels.
4. In a small saucepan, combine tamarind paste, palm sugar, and fish sauce. Cook over medium heat until the sugar dissolves and the sauce thickens slightly.
5. Place fried eggs on a serving platter. Spoon the tamarind sauce over the eggs.
6. Garnish with thinly sliced shallots, chopped roasted peanuts, fresh cilantro leaves, and red chilli slices before serving.

Serving Suggestion: Enjoy hot as an appetiser or side dish with steamed jasmine rice.

62. Vietnamese Bánh Mì with Fried Egg:

- Preparation Time: 15 minutes
- Cooking Time: 15 minutes
- Serves: 4

Ingredients:
- 4 large eggs
- 4 Vietnamese baguettes (bánh mì), split lengthwise
- 1/2 cup mayonnaise
- 1/4 cup

Vietnamese pâté
- 1 cucumber, thinly sliced
- 1 carrot, julienned
- 1/4 cup pickled daikon and carrots (đồ chua)
- Fresh cilantro sprigs
- Maggi seasoning sauce or soy sauce for drizzling
- Chili sauce for serving (optional)

Instructions:
1. Heat a little vegetable oil in a skillet over medium heat. Crack the eggs into the skillet and fry until the whites are set but the yolks are still runny. Remove from the skillet and set aside.
2. Spread mayonnaise and Vietnamese pâté on the split baguettes.
3. Layer cucumber slices, julienned carrot, and pickled daikon and carrots on the bottom halves of the baguettes.
4. Place a fried egg on top of the vegetables on each baguette.
5. Garnish with fresh cilantro sprigs.
6. Drizzle with Maggi seasoning sauce or soy sauce and chilli sauce if desired.

7. Cover with the top halves of the baguettes.
8. Serve immediately.

Serving Suggestion: Enjoy as a delicious and filling breakfast or lunch sandwich.

63. Indian Egg Korma:

- Preparation Time: 20 minutes
- Cooking Time: 30 minutes
- Serves: 4

Ingredients:
- 6 hard-boiled eggs
- 1 onion, chopped
- 2 tomatoes, chopped
- 2 green chilies, chopped
- 1/2 cup cashews
- 1/4 cup yoghourt
- 2 tablespoons vegetable oil
- 1 teaspoon cumin seeds
- 1 teaspoon ginger-garlic paste
- 1 teaspoon ground coriander
- 1/2 teaspoon ground turmeric
- 1/2 teaspoon garam masala
- Salt to taste
- Fresh cilantro leaves for garnish

Instructions:
1. Heat vegetable oil in a skillet over medium heat. Add cumin seeds and let them splutter.
2. Add chopped onion and sauté until golden brown.
3. Add chopped tomatoes and green chilies to the skillet. Cook until the tomatoes are soft.
4. In a blender, combine cashews and yoghurt. Blend until smooth.

5. Add ginger-garlic paste, ground coriander, ground turmeric, and garam masala to the skillet. Cook for another minute.

6. Pour the cashew-yoghourt mixture into the skillet. Cook until the oil separates from the masala.

7. Add hard-boiled eggs to the skillet. Simmer for 5-10 minutes, allowing the flavours to meld together.

8. Season with salt to taste.

9. Garnish with fresh cilantro leaves before serving.

Serving Suggestion: Serve hot with steamed rice or Indian bread like naan or roti.

64. Turkish Börek with Egg:

- Preparation Time: 30 minutes
- Cooking Time: 40 minutes
- Serves: 6

Ingredients:
- 6 large eggs
- 10 phyllo pastry sheets
- 1 cup feta cheese, crumbled
- 1 cup spinach, chopped
- 1/2 cup parsley, chopped
- 1/4 cup olive oil
- Salt and pepper to taste
- Sesame seeds for sprinkling

Instructions:
1. Preheat the oven to 350°F (175°C). Grease a baking dish with olive oil.

2. In a mixing bowl, beat 4 eggs and combine with crumbled feta cheese, chopped spinach, chopped parsley, salt, and pepper.

3. Layer 5 phyllo pastry sheets in the prepared baking dish, brushing each sheet with olive oil.

4. Spread the egg and spinach mixture evenly over the phyllo pastry.

5. Crack the remaining 2 eggs over the filling.

6. Layer the remaining 5 phyllo pastry sheets over the filling, brushing each sheet with olive oil.

7. Sprinkle sesame seeds over the top layer.

8. Bake in the preheated oven for 35-40 minutes, until golden brown and crispy.

9. Allow to cool slightly before slicing and serving.

Serving Suggestion: Serve warm as a savoury breakfast or appetiser with a side salad.

65. French Croque Madame:

- Preparation Time: 15 minutes
- Cooking Time: 10 minutes
- Serves: 2

Ingredients:
- 4 slices of bread
- 4 slices of ham
- 4 slices of Swiss cheese
- 2 tablespoons butter
- 2 large eggs
- Salt and pepper to taste
- Dijon mustard for spreading
- Fresh parsley for garnish

Instructions:
1. Preheat a skillet or griddle over medium heat.

2. Spread Dijon mustard on two slices of bread.

3. Top each mustard-covered slice with 2 slices of ham and 2 slices of Swiss cheese.

4. Place the remaining slices of bread on top to form sandwiches.

5. Melt butter in the preheated skillet or griddle.

6. Place the sandwiches in the skillet and cook until golden brown on both sides and the cheese is melted.

7. In a separate skillet, fry the eggs until the whites are set but the yolks are still runny.

8. Place each sandwich on a plate and top with a fried egg.

9. Season with salt and pepper to taste and garnish with fresh parsley.

Serving Suggestion: Serve hot with a side of mixed greens or French fries.

66. Nigerian Moi Moi (Steamed Bean Pudding with Egg):

- Preparation Time: 20 minutes (plus soaking time)
- Cooking Time: 1 hour
- Serves: 6

Ingredients:
- 2 cups black-eyed peas, soaked overnight
- 1 onion, chopped
- 2 red bell peppers, chopped
- 2 tomatoes, chopped
- 2 cloves garlic
- 1/2 cup vegetable oil
- 2 cups vegetable broth
- 4 hard-boiled eggs, peeled
- Salt and pepper to taste
- Banana leaves or aluminium foil for wrapping

Instructions:
1. Drain and rinse the soaked black-eyed peas.

2. In a blender, combine black-eyed peas, chopped onion, chopped red bell peppers, chopped tomatoes, and garlic. Blend until smooth, adding vegetable broth as needed to achieve a smooth consistency.

3. Transfer the blended mixture to a mixing bowl. Stir in vegetable oil and season with salt and pepper to taste.

4. Cut the hard-boiled eggs in half lengthwise.

5. Line small bowls or ramekins with banana leaves or aluminium foil.

6. Pour the bean mixture into the lined bowls until halfway full. Place a halved hard-boiled egg in the centre of each bowl, cut side down.

7. Fill the bowls with more bean mixture until the eggs are covered.

8. Cover the bowls tightly with banana leaves or aluminium foil.

9. Steam the moi moi in a steamer or large pot with a steaming rack for 1 hour, until firm and cooked through.

10. Allow to cool slightly before serving.

Serving Suggestion: Serve warm as a main dish or side dish with rice or bread.

67. Egyptian Hawawshi with Egg:

- Preparation Time: 30 minutes
- Cooking Time: 40 minutes
- Serves: 4

Ingredients:
- 4 large eggs
- 1 lb ground beef or lamb
- 1 onion, finely chopped
- 2 tomatoes, finely chopped
- 2 green chilies, seeded and chopped
- 2 cloves garlic, minced

- 1 teaspoon ground cumin
- 1 teaspoon ground coriander
- 1/2 teaspoon paprika
- Salt and pepper to taste
- 4 pita bread rounds
- Vegetable oil for frying

Instructions:
1. Preheat the oven to 375°F (190°C).
2. In a mixing bowl, combine ground beef or lamb with chopped onion, chopped tomatoes, chopped green chilies, minced garlic, ground cumin, ground coriander, paprika, salt, and pepper.
3. Cut each pita bread round in half to form pockets.
4. Stuff each pita bread pocket with the meat mixture, pressing down to compact.
5. Heat vegetable oil in a skillet over medium heat. Fry the stuffed pita bread pockets on both sides until golden brown and crispy.
6. Transfer the fried hawawshi to a baking sheet.
7. Crack an egg onto the centre of each hawawshi.
8. Bake in the preheated oven for 10-15 minutes, until the egg whites are set but the yolks are still runny.
9. Serve hot.

Serving Suggestion: Enjoy with a side of tahini sauce or yoghurt sauce.

68. Lebanese Knafeh with Egg:

- Preparation Time: 30 minutes
- Cooking Time: 45 minutes
- Serves: 8

Ingredients:
- 4 large eggs
- 1 lb kadayif (shredded phyllo dough)
- 1 cup unsalted butter, melted
- 2 cups akkawi cheese, shredded
- 1/2 cup sugar
- 1/4 cup rose water
- 1/4 cup orange blossom water
- Pistachios, chopped, for garnish

Syrup:
- 2 cups sugar
- 1 cup water
- 1 tablespoon lemon juice

Instructions:
1. Preheat the oven to 350°F (175°C). Grease a baking dish with butter.
2. In a mixing bowl, combine shredded phyllo dough with melted butter, mixing until well coated.
3. Spread half of the phyllo dough mixture in the prepared baking dish, pressing down firmly to form a crust.
4. Spread shredded akkawi cheese evenly over the phyllo dough crust.
5. In a separate mixing bowl, beat eggs with sugar, rose water, and orange blossom water until well combined.
6. Pour the egg mixture over the cheese layer in the baking dish.
7. Spread the remaining half of the phyllo dough mixture over the egg layer, pressing down gently.

8. Bake in the preheated oven for 40-45 minutes, until golden brown and crispy.

9. While the knafeh is baking, prepare the syrup by combining sugar, water, and lemon juice in a saucepan. Bring to a boil, then reduce heat and simmer for 10 minutes, until slightly thickened.

10. Once the knafeh is baked, pour the hot syrup evenly over the hot knafeh.

11. Garnish with chopped pistachios before serving.

Serving Suggestion: Serve hot or at room temperature as a sweet dessert or snack.

69. Spanish Patatas a la Riojana with Egg:

- Preparation Time: 20 minutes
- Cooking Time: 40 minutes
- Serves: 4

Ingredients:
- 4 large eggs
- 4 potatoes, peeled and diced
- 1 onion, chopped
- 2 cloves garlic, minced
- 2 chorizo sausages, sliced
- 2 cups chicken broth
- 1/2 teaspoon smoked paprika
- Salt and pepper to taste
- Olive oil for frying
- Fresh parsley, chopped, for garnish

Instructions:
1. Heat olive oil in a large skillet or pot over medium heat. Add chopped onion and minced garlic. Cook until softened.

2. Add diced potatoes to the skillet and cook until lightly golden brown.

3. Stir in sliced chorizo sausages and smoked paprika. Cook for another 2-3 minutes.

4. Pour chicken broth into the skillet, ensuring the potatoes are submerged. Bring to a boil, then reduce heat and simmer for 20-25 minutes, until the potatoes are tender and the flavors are melded together.

5. While the potatoes are cooking, heat a little olive oil in a separate skillet over medium heat. Fry the eggs until the whites are set but the yolks are still runny.

6. Once the potatoes are cooked, season with salt and pepper to taste.

7. Divide the potato and chorizo mixture into serving bowls. Top each bowl with a fried egg.

8. Garnish with chopped fresh parsley before serving.

Serving Suggestion: Serve hot with crusty bread for a hearty and satisfying meal.

70. Thai Khai Khem (Salted Eggs):

- Preparation Time: 10 minutes
- Cooking Time: 20 days (including curing time)
- Makes: 4 salted eggs

Ingredients:
- 4 large duck eggs (or chicken eggs)
- 2 cups salt
- 4 cups water

Instructions:
1. In a large pot, dissolve salt in water to create a brine solution.

2. Carefully place the eggs in the brine solution, ensuring they are fully submerged.

3. Cover the pot and let the eggs soak in the brine for 20 days at room temperature.

4. After 20 days, remove the eggs from the brine and gently rinse them under cold water.

5. Pat the eggs dry with paper towels and store them in the refrigerator.

6. To use, crack open the salted eggs and use the salted egg yolks in various dishes.

Serving Suggestion: Serve salted eggs as a condiment or ingredient in dishes such as Thai fried rice or Chinese mooncakes.

71. Brazilian Brigadeiro with Egg:

- Preparation Time: 10 minutes
- Cooking Time: 20 minutes
- Makes: 20 brigadeiros

Ingredients:
- 1 can (14 oz) sweetened condensed milk
- 3 tablespoons unsweetened cocoa powder
- 1 tablespoon butter
- Chocolate sprinkles for coating

Instructions:
1. In a non-stick saucepan, combine sweetened condensed milk, cocoa powder, and butter.

2. Cook the mixture over medium heat, stirring constantly, until it thickens and pulls away from the sides of the pan (about 10-15 minutes).

3. Remove the mixture from heat and let it cool to room temperature.

4. Once cooled, grease your hands with butter and roll the mixture into small balls.

5. Roll the brigadeiros in chocolate sprinkles to coat evenly.

6. Place the brigadeiros in small paper cups.

7. Serve at room temperature or chilled.

Serving Suggestion: Serve brigadeiros as a sweet treat at parties or celebrations.

72. Mexican Tlacoyo with Egg:

- Preparation Time: 30 minutes
- Cooking Time: 30 minutes
- Serves: 4

Ingredients:
- 1 cup masa harina (corn flour)
- 1/2 cup warm water
- 1 cup refried beans
- 1 cup crumbled queso fresco (or feta cheese)
- 4 large eggs
- Vegetable oil for frying
- Salsa, avocado slices, and chopped cilantro for serving

Instructions:

1. In a mixing bowl, combine masa harina with warm water to form a soft dough. Divide the dough into 4 equal portions.

2. Flatten each portion of dough into oval-shaped disks.

3. Spread a layer of refried beans onto each masa disk, leaving a border around the edges.

4. Fold the masa disk over the filling to form a half-moon shape and pinch the edges to seal.

5. Heat vegetable oil in a skillet over medium heat. Fry the tlacoyos until golden brown and crispy on both sides (about 3-4 minutes per side).

6. Remove the tlacoyos from the skillet and drain on paper towels.

7. In the same skillet, fry the eggs to desired doneness (fried or scrambled).

8. To serve, place a fried egg on top of each tlacoyo.

9. Garnish with salsa, avocado slices, and chopped cilantro.

Serving Suggestion: Serve tlacoyos with egg as a hearty breakfast or brunch dish.

73. Italian Eggplant Caponata:

- Preparation Time: 20 minutes
- Cooking Time: 30 minutes
- Serves: 6

Ingredients:
- 2 large eggplants, diced
- 1 onion, diced
- 2 cloves garlic, minced
- 2 tomatoes, diced
- 1/4 cup olive oil
- 2 tablespoons red wine vinegar
- 2 tablespoons capers, drained
- 1/4 cup green olives, sliced
- 2 tablespoons pine nuts
- 1 tablespoon sugar
- Salt and pepper to taste
- Fresh basil leaves for garnish

Instructions:
1. Heat olive oil in a large skillet over medium heat. Add diced eggplants and cook until golden brown and softened.

2. Remove the cooked eggplants from the skillet and set aside.

3. In the same skillet, add diced onion and minced garlic. Cook until softened.

4. Add diced tomatoes, red wine vinegar, capers, sliced olives, pine nuts, and sugar to the skillet. Cook until the tomatoes are softened and the mixture thickens slightly.

5. Return the cooked eggplants to the skillet and stir to combine with the tomato mixture.

6. Season with salt and pepper to taste.

7. Simmer the caponata for an additional 10-15 minutes to allow the flavours to meld together.

8. Garnish with fresh basil leaves before serving.

Serving Suggestion: Serve eggplant caponata as a side dish or appetiser with crusty bread or crackers.

74. Nigerian Akara (Bean Fritters with Egg):

- Preparation Time: 20 minutes (plus soaking time)
- Cooking Time: 20 minutes
- Serves: 4

Ingredients:
- 2 cups black-eyed peas, soaked overnight
- 1 onion, chopped
- 2 cloves garlic, minced
- 2 tablespoons red bell pepper, chopped
- 2 tablespoons green bell pepper, chopped
- 1 teaspoon ground cayenne pepper (optional)
- Salt to taste
- Vegetable oil for frying
- Hard-boiled eggs, sliced, for serving

Instructions:
1. Drain and rinse the soaked black-eyed peas. Transfer to a blender or food processor.

2. Add chopped onion, minced garlic, chopped red and green bell peppers, ground cayenne pepper (if using), and salt to the blender with the black-eyed peas. Blend until smooth, adding a little water if needed to achieve a thick batter consistency.

3. Heat vegetable oil in a deep fryer or skillet over medium heat.

4. Drop spoonfuls of the bean batter into the hot oil and fry until golden brown and crispy on all sides (about 3-4 minutes per side).

5. Remove the fried bean fritters from the oil and drain on paper towels.

6. Serve the akara fritters with sliced hard-boiled eggs.

Serving Suggestion: Serve akara with egg as a protein-rich breakfast or snack.

75. Lebanese Manakish with Egg:

- Preparation Time: 30 minutes
- Cooking Time: 15 minutes
- Serves: 4

Ingredients:
Dough:
- 2 cups all-purpose flour
- 1 teaspoon instant yeast
- 1 teaspoon sugar
- 1/2 teaspoon salt
- 3/4 cup warm water
- 2 tablespoons olive oil

Topping:
- 4 eggs
- 1/2 cup za'atar spice mix
- 2 tablespoons olive oil

Instructions:

1. In a mixing bowl, combine all-purpose flour, instant yeast, sugar, and salt. Gradually add warm water and olive oil, mixing until a smooth dough forms.

2. Knead the dough on a floured surface for 5-7 minutes, until elastic.

3. Place the dough in a greased bowl, cover with a clean kitchen towel, and let it rise in a warm place for 1 hour, until doubled in size.

4. Preheat the oven to 425°F (220°C). Line a baking sheet with parchment paper.

5. Punch down the risen dough and divide it into 4 equal portions. Roll out each portion into a round circle.

6. Place the dough rounds on the prepared baking sheet.

7. Spread za'atar spice mix evenly over each dough round.

8. Crack an egg into the centre of each dough round.

9. Drizzle olive oil over the eggs and around the edges of the dough.

10. Bake in the preheated oven for 12-15 minutes, until the crust is golden brown and the eggs are cooked to desired doneness.

11. Remove from the oven and let cool slightly before serving.

Serving Suggestion: Serve manakish with egg as a flavorful breakfast or snack, accompanied by fresh vegetables and labneh.

76. Korean Kimchi Fried Rice with Egg:

- Preparation Time: 15 minutes
- Cooking Time: 15 minutes
- Serves: 2

Ingredients:
- 2 cups cooked rice, preferably day-old
- 1 cup kimchi, chopped
- 2 tablespoons kimchi juice
- 2 eggs
- 2 green onions, thinly sliced
- 2 tablespoons soy sauce
- 1 tablespoon sesame oil
- 1 tablespoon vegetable oil
- Salt and pepper to taste
- Sesame seeds for garnish

Instructions:
1. Heat vegetable oil in a large skillet or wok over medium heat.
2. Add chopped kimchi to the skillet and stir-fry for 2-3 minutes.
3. Add cooked rice to the skillet and stir-fry with the kimchi for another 3-4 minutes.
4. Stir in soy sauce, kimchi juice, and sesame oil. Mix well to combine.
5. Push the kimchi fried rice to one side of the skillet and crack the eggs into the empty side.
6. Scramble the eggs until cooked through, then mix them into the fried rice.
7. Season with salt and pepper to taste.
8. Garnish with sliced green onions and sesame seeds before serving.

77. Thai Pad See Ew with Egg:

- Preparation Time: 20 minutes
- Cooking Time: 10 minutes
- Serves: 2

Ingredients:
- 8 oz wide rice noodles
- 2 tablespoons soy sauce
- 1 tablespoon oyster sauce
- 1 tablespoon fish sauce
- 1 tablespoon brown sugar
- 2 tablespoons vegetable oil
- 2 cloves garlic, minced
- 2 eggs
- 2 cups Chinese broccoli or regular broccoli, chopped
- 1 cup sliced protein of choice (such as chicken, beef, or tofu)
- White pepper to taste

Instructions:
1. Cook the rice noodles according to package instructions. Drain and set aside.
2. In a small bowl, mix together soy sauce, oyster sauce, fish sauce, and brown sugar to make the sauce.
3. Heat vegetable oil in a large skillet or wok over medium-high heat.
4. Add minced garlic to the skillet and stir-fry for 30 seconds.
5. Crack the eggs into the skillet and scramble until cooked through.

6. Add the chopped Chinese broccoli and sliced protein to the skillet. Stir-fry until the broccoli is tender and the protein is cooked.

7. Add the cooked rice noodles to the skillet, followed by the prepared sauce.

8. Stir-fry everything together until well combined and heated through.

9. Season with white pepper to taste.

10. Serve hot.

Serving Suggestion: Serve Pad See Ew with egg as a flavorful Thai street food-inspired dish, garnished with fresh lime wedges and crushed peanuts.

78. Brazilian Pamonha with Egg:

- Preparation Time: 30 minutes
- Cooking Time: 1 hour
- Serves: 6

Ingredients:
- 6 ears of corn, husked and cleaned
- 1 cup milk
- 1/2 cup sugar
- Pinch of salt
- 6 eggs

Instructions:
1. Grate the corn kernels off the cobs using a box grater or blender.

2. In a blender, blend the grated corn kernels with milk, sugar, and salt until smooth.

3. Strain the corn mixture through a fine-mesh sieve to remove any remaining solids.

4. Pour the strained corn mixture into corn husks, folding and tying them securely to form pouches.

5. Place the filled corn husk pouches in a large pot of boiling water and cook for 1 hour.

6. Meanwhile, bring a separate pot of water to a boil and gently lower the eggs into the water. Boil for 8-10 minutes, then remove and let cool before peeling.

7. Once cooked, remove the pamonhas from the water and let them cool slightly before serving.

8. Serve each pamonha with a boiled egg.

Serving Suggestion: Serve pamonha with egg as a traditional Brazilian delicacy, often enjoyed as a snack or breakfast item.

79. Italian Tiramisu:

- Preparation Time: 30 minutes
- Chilling Time: 4 hours
- Serves: 6-8

Ingredients:
- 3 large eggs, separated
- 3/4 cup granulated sugar
- 1 cup mascarpone cheese
- 1 cup heavy cream
- 2 cups brewed espresso, cooled
- 2 tablespoons coffee liqueur (optional)
- 24 ladyfinger cookies
- Cocoa powder for dusting

Instructions:
1. In a mixing bowl, beat egg yolks with sugar until thick and pale yellow.

2. Add mascarpone cheese to the egg yolk mixture and beat until smooth.

3. In a separate mixing bowl, beat egg whites until stiff peaks form.

4. In another bowl, whip heavy cream until stiff peaks form.

5. Gently fold the whipped cream into the mascarpone mixture until well combined.

6. Dip each ladyfinger cookie into the brewed espresso (and coffee liqueur, if using) briefly, then arrange them in the bottom of a serving dish to form a layer.

7. Spread half of the mascarpone mixture over the soaked ladyfingers.

8. Repeat with another layer of soaked ladyfingers and the remaining mascarpone mixture.

9. Cover the dish with plastic wrap and refrigerate for at least 4 hours, or overnight, to set.

10. Before serving, dust the top of the tiramisu with cocoa powder.

Serving Suggestion: Serve tiramisu as a classic Italian dessert, garnished with chocolate shavings or fresh berries.

80. Indian Egg Curry:

- Preparation Time: 15 minutes
- Cooking Time: 30 minutes
- Serves: 4

Ingredients:
- 6 hard-boiled eggs, peeled
- 2 onions, finely chopped
- 2 tomatoes, finely chopped
- 2 green chilies, slit lengthwise
- 1 tablespoon ginger-garlic paste
- 1 teaspoon cumin seeds
- 1 teaspoon coriander powder
- 1/2 teaspoon turmeric powder
- 1/2 teaspoon red chili powder
- 1/2 teaspoon garam masala

- 1/4 cup coconut milk
- 2 tablespoons vegetable oil
- Salt to taste
- Fresh cilantro leaves for garnish

Instructions:
1. Heat vegetable oil in a large skillet or pot over medium heat.
2. Add cumin seeds and let them splutter.
3. Add chopped onions and sauté until golden brown.
4. Add ginger-garlic paste and slit green chilies. Sauté for another minute.
5. Add chopped tomatoes and cook until they turn soft and mushy.
6. Stir in coriander powder, turmeric powder, red chili powder, and salt. Cook the spices for 2-3 minutes.
7. Add coconut milk and simmer for 5 minutes, until the curry thickens slightly.
8. Gently add the hard-boiled eggs to the curry, ensuring they are submerged.
9. Cover and simmer the curry for 10-15 minutes, allowing the flavors to meld together.
10. Sprinkle garam masala over the curry and garnish with fresh cilantro leaves before serving.

Serving Suggestion: Serve egg curry with steamed rice or Indian bread such as naan or roti for a comforting and flavorful meal.

www.ingramcontent.com/pod-product-compliance
Lightning Source LLC
Chambersburg PA
CBHW020624160726
47991CB00002BA/920